GW01605483

Jeremy Taylor
Anglican Theologian

JEREMY TAYLOR
Anglican Theologian

H. R. McAdoo

Foreword:
Rev. Dr. J. K. Carroll

Church of Ireland Historical Society
1997

This lecture, delivered on 9th November 1996
in the Chapter House of Christ Church Cathedral, Dublin,
is published by the Church of Ireland Historical Society
at the request of the members.

A catalogue record for this title is available from the British Library

ISBN 0953 0677 0X

Printed by Graham & Sons (Printers) Ltd., 51 Gortin Road, Omagh, Co. Tyrone Tel: (01662) 249222

Plate 1. Jeremy Taylor, from the portrait at All Souls College, Oxford. Engraved by Peter Lombart, frontispiece from Ductor Dubitantium, first edition, London, 1660. (Armagh Public Library).

FOREWORD

The scientific soul of our brave new world began in the early seventeenth century with its new approaches to reality, but its gradual evolution and modern prejudices are distinctively its own. In the age of Milton and Bacon neither the Word of God nor the words of man were in doubt as to metaphysical significance, although biblical and scientific reality were beginning to be separate, at least in discourse. Today, however there is a crisis in the concept and understanding of language itself that tells of our incapacity to express in words humanity's innermost truths, sensory experiences, moral and transcendent intuitions. Jeremy Taylor, (called *Anglican Theologian* in Dr McAdoo's lecture, and described in his epitaph in Dromore Cathedral as *erudite theologian, renowned preacher and faithful pastor)* is relevant to our atheistic and deconstructionist times. This was not because he lived in a century that resembled ours in its political, religious and philosophical upheavals, but because in that age he lived and moved and had his being in the eternal Word of God, made new by the scriptural zeal of the Reformers, and renewed still more by the Caroline appeal to tradition, and to reason.

In the Caroline renewal, or appeal to the early Church when *Catholicism* referred more to the fulness of revelation than to the universality of an institution, the scholar-bishop was born again, so to speak, and names like Lancelot Andrews, William Laud, and John Cosin began to flourish in England. In Ireland, John Bramhall, James Ussher and Jeremy Taylor are but the first names in a litany that is long and living. Nourished and moulded by the being and texture of the *King James Bible*, as the Latin Fathers were by the *Vulgate,* and the Greek Fathers had been by the *Septuagint,* those scholar-bishops are the English Fathers of a spirituality and a theology that is the "Great Code" of our literary and cultural heritage.

In my opinion Jeremy Taylor was the first of those Carolines, and for that matter of Renaissance theologians in general, to grasp in a metaphysical manner the symbolic nature of language and reality in the world of the early Greek and Latin Fathers. In these circumstances the biblical word simply gave a new ontological significance to symbolic reality. The sacramental order quite naturally came into being for those who had eyes in their souls to see and ears in their hearts to hear. Consequently, in his voluminous writings, words and images of the ancient faith like *mystery, sacrament, figure, symbol, similitude, type and representation* came to new life and meaning, as if incarnating a real and true presence of significant being in an age that was more scientific than metaphysical, more symbolic in an unreal sense than sacramental in a real sense. Thus in Taylor's theology of *sacramental representation* our horizons are broadened, and "the heavenly sacrifice" and "the earthly sacraments" are once again made one, and the divisions of Trent and the Reformers are overcome:

> Now what Christ does in heaven, He had commanded us to do on earth, that is to represent his death, to commemorate this sacrifice by humble prayer and thankful record; and by faithful manifestation and joyful eucharist to lay it before the eyes of our heavenly Father, so ministering in his priesthood, and doing according to His commandment and His example; the Church being the image of heaven, the priest the minister of Christ; the holy table being a copy of the celestial altar, and the external holy table being a copy of the celestial altar, and the eternal sacrifice of the lamb slain from the beginning of the world being always the same; it bleeds no more after the finishing of it on the cross; but it is wonderfully represented in heaven and graciously represented here; by Christ's action there and by His commandment here.(1)

This sacramental vision of Christ and the Church, of worship and the world, explains the "interlocking of themes" and the "underlying unity of thought" which Dr McAdoo finds in Taylor's varied works, and which he calls "a vein of moral/ascetic theology and a vein of sacramental theology, which merge and undergird all that (Taylor) writes".(2) In fact, the selection from Taylor's works, made for the volume on Jeremy Taylor in the *Classics of Western Spirituality* series, was structured and presented in its chapter divisions to illustrate in its theological unity the McAdoo theses: hence, 1. Jesus Christ - The Great Exemplar; 2. The Heavenly Sacrifice and the Earthly Sacraments; 3. Faith and Repentance; 4. Sermon, Discourse and Prayer; 5. Holy Living and Holy Dying.(3)

This vision of faith more than of dogma pervades Dr McAdoo's recent writings on Taylor, and on the Anglican heritage in general, and is characterized by him as "a spirituality of the five Ds: devotion, duty, discipline, detail and doctrine".(4) For Dr McAdoo, as for Dr Taylor, theology and spirituality are about men and women transformed into a new nature - the genuine human being of Irenaeus - 'born again', and "called by the apostle *the apaugasma tou theou*; Christ is this *brightness of God* manifested in the hearts of His dearest servants".(5) To the extent that such spiritual men and women exist in the hierarchical Churches to that extent are our Churches being renewed and reunion is being accomplished, as mysteriously as the increase that is given in growth. This renewed emphasis in Dr McAdoo's approach is of much ecumenical significance for, like the Exodus, it takes us out of ourselves and our institutions, and, like the Covenant, it brings us into the world of Mystery and Sacrament that is God's real presence among us. Here, all can be at one in grateful thanksgiving, and can celebrate in season and out of season the unity and the grace of renewal that is already present, and the much more that is yet to come through the goodwill of renewal and the renewal of goodwill:

> For when our reason is raised up by the Spirit of Christ, it is turned quickly into experience; when our faith relies upon the principles of Christ, it is changed into vision. And so long as we know God only in the ways of man, by contentious learning, by arguing and dispute, we see nothing but the shadow of Him, and in that shadow we meet with many dark appearances, little certainty, and much conjecture. But when we know Him with the eyes of holiness, and the intuition of gracious experience, with a quiet spirit and the peace of enjoyment, then we shall hear what we never heard and see what our eyes never saw; then the mysteries of godliness shall be opened unto us, and clear as the windows of the morning.(6)

These primordial words, like those of a poet, are filled with the soft music of infinity: spoken by Taylor, preacher and priest, such words are sacramental and communicate directly to the soul a presence that is transcendent and real. Taylor's voluminous writings tell of this presence, which becomes on every page a possession, a pleasure and a prayer. Indeed there is scarcely a writer in the tradition of English spirituality since Taylor or before him whose words reveal with so much music and peace the secret of God's love in man's heart:

> But I shall say no more of this at this time, for this is to be felt and not talked of . . . All that I shall now say of it is, that a good man is united unto God, as a flame touches a flame, and combines into splendour and to glory: so is the spirit of a man united unto Christ by the Spirit of God.(7)

T. K. CARROLL

(1) Carroll, T.K. *Jeremy Taylor*, Selected Works, *Classics of Western Spirituality* series; Paulist Press, N.J. 1990. p.209. Quotation from *The Worthy Communicant*, Heber-Eden, V.8

(2) McAdoo, H.R. *The Eucharistic Theology of Jeremy Taylor Today*, Canterbury Press, Norwich, 1988, p.14

(3) Carroll, T.K. op. cit.

(4) McAdoo, H.R & Stevenson, K. *The Mystery of the Eucharist in the Anglican Tradition,* Canterbury Press, Norwich, 1995, p.52

(5) Carroll, T.K. Op. Cit. P.376. Quotation from Sermon *VI, Via Intelligentiae*, Heber-Eden, V.8

(6) ibid

(7) ibid

LIFE OF JEREMY TAYLOR 1613-1667

1613	born Cambridge
1626	enters Gonville and Caius
1633	Fellow of Gonville and Caius; ordained (no record survives)
1635	Fellow All Souls Oxford. Chaplain to the King (due to patronage of Archbishop Laud)
1638	Rector of Uppingham marries Phoebe Landisdale
1642	Civil War; chaplain with Royal Army; awarded D.D. by King's command publishes *Episcopacy Asserted* captured by Parliamentarians
1645	takes refuge in Wales with Lord Carbery at Golden Grove
1647	*Liberty of Prophesying* a plea for religious tolerance
1649	*Great Exemplar* a life of Christ "first of its kind"
1650	*Holy Living*
1651	*Holy Dying* death of his wife
1654	Preaching in London defending Prayer Book and encouraging royalists; short imprisonments
1655	marries Joanna Bridges. *Unum Necessarium* doctrine of repentance source of much controversy
1658	to avoid imprisonment brought by Lord Conway to Lisnagarvey (Lisburn)
1660	*Ductor Dubitantium* cases of conscience *The Worthy Communicant*
	Vice Chancellor Trinity College Dublin, sent by Duke of Ormonde to restore the College to Anglicanism.
1661	consecrated Bishop of Down, Connor and Dromore in St. Patrick's Dublin. Preacher at the service where two Archbishops and ten Bishops were consecrated.
	rebuilds Dromore Cathedral involved in bitter disputes to remove Presbyterian ministers from Church of Ireland parishes.
1665	builds Ballinderry Church
1666	death of only remaining son
1667	death at Lisburn

LIST OF PLATES

Plate 2. Frontispiece, engraved by William Faithorne for the eighth edition of The Great Exemplar. A life of Jesus, first published in 1649. London, 1703. (Armagh Public Library).

Plate 3. The Goodly Cedar of Apostolic and Catholic Episcopacy...17th century engraving. (Armagh Public Library).

JEREMY TAYLOR

ANGLICAN THEOLOGIAN

The title of this lecture must not mislead you into thinking that Taylor is typical in the sense of being 'a typical Anglican theologian' whatever shade of meaning you may attach to that phrase. For though Taylor was robustly and devotedly Anglican at a time when that loyalty cost him dear, he cannot be type-cast. His theology is as profound as his reach was wide but in many respects, as I hope to show, he resists classification. He stands out in a century starred with great names and as expounding an orthodoxy which envelopes a liberality of spirit and a graced independence of mind as he proclaims the faith 'once for all delivered'. This he does with a loving but sometimes critical assessment of aspects of the great tradition from the patristic past in which like so many of his contemporaries, he is steeped. He possesses a unique quality, hard to define but easily experienced.

THE MAN IS THE STYLE

But before I try to substantiate this I would recall to you that we are looking at a most attractive human being with an enormous range of interests but who all the time comes across in his writings, as he did to his friends, with a warmth of feeling and an empathy to which one can instantly relate. His first modern editor, Reginald Heber registered this in 1822, concluding his life of Taylor with the sentence 'Hooker is the object of our reverence, Barrow of our admiration, and Jeremy Taylor of our love'. For Heber, this is because Taylor 'persuades and delights most' and it is 'this distinctive excellence, still more than the other qualifications of learning and logical acuteness, which has placed him, even in that age of gigantic talent, on an eminence superior to any of his immediate contemporaries'.(1) Similarly, Sir Edmund Gosse in 1904, composing his Life of Taylor, yielded to the same quality in his subject, – a quality too deeply devotional and too profoundly human to be designated 'charm', – when he described him as 'the most gracious voice then to be heard in England'.(2) In our own time, C. J. Stranks concurred that 'the man himself was as gracious as his works'.(3)

PORTRAIT BY A FRIEND

Fortunately for us, we have first-hand evidence from one who knew Taylor well and who worked with him in Ireland. George Rust, recommended to Taylor by his old friend the Cambridge Platonist Henry More, was appointed Dean of Connor and subsequently succeeded as Bishop of Dromore of which small diocese Taylor had been administrator. (4) In one of his letters, Worthington, to whom we owed the edition of the *Discourses* of Smith, the Cambridge Platonist, calls Rust 'an excellent person . . . Mr Rust, is going over into Ireland, to be Dean of Down, being invited thither by Dr. Taylor, the Bishop', (John Worthington, *Miscellanies,* VI). The cathedral of Christ the Redeemer, Dromore, ruined during the rebellion of 1641, was rebuilt by Taylor who himself paid for the chancel. The communion plate was the gift of Joanna Taylor, either his wife or his daughter. Paradoxically, it is from Rust's funeral sermon that we capture the only full portrait from life of Jeremy Taylor,(5) though he appears in the *Diary* of John Evelyn, a close friend, who chose him as his spiritual adviser. Not only does Rust's friendship and work-relationship with Taylor make the strokes of the portrait authentic and realist but we bear in mind that Rust was speaking to those who knew Taylor personally and as their bishop. We are thus preserved from that kind of hagiography in which distance lends enchantment. Joseph Glanville, who edited Rust's *Discourses* (1682) had the highest opinion of him as a theologian and scholar but also as a man. His description of Rust reveals a temperament very similar to that of Taylor: 'of a free understanding and vast capacity joined with singular modesty and an unusual sweetness of temper which made him the darling of all that knew him'.

When we turn to Rust's characterization of Taylor we can see that it was a case of like calling to like. Intellectually, spiritually and ecclesiastically they were clearly *simpatico* and Glanville's picture of Rust as a man of great piety and generosity, a profound philosopher and 'close reasoner . . . who had all the qualifications of a primitive Bishop' mirrors Rust's own assessment of his great contemporary and colleague. Historians will know of Taylor's courage in his imprisonments and in his personal bereavements, his ejectment from his parish of Uppingham, his exile in Wales where to support his family he set up a school with his fellow-victim of persecution William Nicholson the deprived Archdeacon of Brecon, and his poverty which never dimmed his faith or his commitment to a despoiled and almost dismantled Church. Likewise, theologians are familiar with the astounding spread of his expertise and the amazing industry with which in such conditions he produced significant book after significant book. Rust touches on both these aspects but it is with his pen-picture of Taylor the man that I am immediately concerned because what Taylor was comes through so clearly in his writings. 'His worth' said Rust 'is much greater than his fame; it is impossible not to speak great things of him, and yet it is impossible to speak what he deserves'.(6)

HIS LITERARY GENIUS

Quite literally the man is the style just as the style is the man and this, I believe, is the explanation of why Taylor's writings are able to create the imaginative nexus between him and the reader which Heber, Gosse and Stranks experienced. Their experience was duplicated for Coleridge who reckoned Taylor as a literary figure 'four square, each against each' with Shakespeare, Milton and Bacon. The reaction of Charles Lamb and Hazlitt was the same and in the 1930's Logan Pearsall Smith wrote of the magic of style in Taylor when, varying from a graceful Ciceronian style, Taylor then 'seems to dip his pen in enchanted ink; the words begin to dance and glitter, and a splendour falls upon the illuminated page' and 'an imagination radiant and strange, seems to unfold its wings and soar aloft'. Speaking as one who for half a century has been a willing prisoner of Taylor's genius and theological versatility, I feel that Logan Pearsall Smith put his finger on what creates this empathy between generations of readers and Taylor himself when he pointed out that style in Taylor is no technical trick or mere literary adornment. Rather is it 'like the colouring of a painter, a quality of the writer's vision . . . It is Jeremy Taylor's possession of style in this sense, the revelation in the music and magic of words of a unique vision – it is this rarest of gifts which we value in him'.(7) As I said, it is the inner man himself expressed in his thoughts and captured in his words who comes through and enfolds the reader in the spirituality and warmth of his religion and his perception of the human condition.

To me, it is very striking that this too was how George Rust saw, knew and valued him during Taylor's lifetime. 'Nature had befriended him much in his constitution' he writes

> 'for he was a person of most sweet and obliging humour, of great candour and ingenuity; and there was so much of salt and fineness of wit, and prettiness of address, in his familiar discourses, as made his conversation have all the pleasantness of a comedy, and all the usefulness of a sermon. His soul was made up of harmony; and he never spake, but he charmed his hearer, not only with the clearness of his reason, but all his words, and his very tone and cadences, were strangely harmonical'.

Not only had Taylor a lovely voice but his looks were striking and his manner winning. Rust speaks of 'his florid and youthful beauty, and sweet and pleasant air' in his young days, but he discerns that fusion of the man and the style which I have remarked on as being the source of Taylor's attractiveness to subsequent generations both as a person and as a writer:

> 'But that which did most of all captivate and enravish, was, the gaiety and richness of fancy; for he had much in him of that natural enthusiasm, that inspires all great poets and orators; and there was a generous ferment in his blood and spirits, that set his fancy bravely a-work, and made it swell, and teem, and become pregnant to such degrees of luxuriancy, as nothing but the greatness of his wit and judgment, could have kept it within due bounds and measures'.

This, I would suggest, is perfectly illustrated in Taylor's *The Great Exemplar* (1649), the first ever life of Christ in English, in which the *Narrative* is written in a lucid style, its music in a subdued key, while the *Considerations* are in a style that is delicate, brilliant, sensitively imaginative – recalling Logan Pearsall Smith's 'enchanted ink' and Gosse's 'richness of imaginative ornament'. Yet again when the book turns to the *Discourses* we meet the simplicity and practicality of the moral theologian who insists that we must 'make religion to be our work', 'the business of our lives'. This variation in style is deliberate, as Taylor himself says, pointing out that he seeks to match manner with matter, and to keep alert the reader's interest.

COUNSELLOR AND INDEPENDENT THINKER

With equal clarity of discernment, Rust notes this basic concern as a spiritual adviser when he comments on Taylor's skill in 'casuistical divinity; and he was a rare conductor of souls, and knew how to counsel and to advise; to solve difficulties, and determine cases, and quiet consciences'. While I hold that Taylor is primarily a moral/ascetical theologian, I believe the great range of his theology and the spirit in which he did theology are equally noteworthy. That perceptive man, Rust, spotted this when having commented on Taylor's 'mighty industry' and his books 'enough of themselves to furnish a library', he goes straight to the heart, the methodology of Taylor as a theologian who was 'a zealous son of the Church of England . . . that he would never be governed by anything but reason, and the evidence of truth'.

The passage which follows is, I think, essential to the understanding of Taylor as a positive Anglican theologian and as a creative religious thinker whose individuality will not permit him to be pigeon-holed:

> 'Indeed, it was a rare mixture and a single instance, hardly to be found in an age: for the great trier of wits has told us, that there is a peculiar and several complexion, required for wit, and judgment, and fancy; and yet you might have found all these in this great personage, in their eminency and perfection'.

Rust then goes on to enlarge on what I have called the liberality which one meets constantly in Taylor's huge output. 'Liberality' is the late Alec Vidler's term by which he meant 'the opposite not of conservative, but of fanatical or bigoted or intransigent. It points to the *esprit large* and away from the *idée fixe*'.(8) You will note this very term, *esprit large*, in the passage from Rust:

> 'But that which made his wit and judgment so considerable, was *the largeness and freedom of his spirit*; for truth is plain and easy to a mind disentangled from superstition and prejudice; he was one of the *eklektikoi*, a sort of brave philosophers . . . that did not addict themselves to any particular sect, but ingeniously sought for truth among all the wrangling schools . . . This was the spirit of this great man; he weighed men's reasons and not their names . . . He considered that it is not likely any one party should wholly engross truth to themselves; that obedience is the only way to true knowledge'.

It can, I think, be demonstrated that this quality runs like a golden thread through all Taylor's handling of the different fields of theology which he investigates.

PASTOR AND INTELLECTUAL

But I must finish with George Rust's portrait from life and attempt some sort of sketch of Taylor as one of the great ornaments of Anglican theology. Suffice it to say that Rust, speaking as I said to those who knew – 'We are all his witnesses' – put on record Taylor's wide learning in patristics, in scholastic theology and also 'he was a rare humanist, and hugely versed in all the polite parts of learning . . . the ancient moralists, Greek and Roman . . . and . . . the refined wits of later ages, whether French or Italian'. Above all he called to his hearers' minds Taylor's humility, 'his solemn hours of prayer' and that he 'was courteous and affable, and of easy access'. He records too 'his large and diffusive charity', noting how little was left in his estate because Taylor who knew want and poverty (John Evelyn had to help him financially) allowed 'charity (to be) the steward for a great proportion of his revenue'. It is a portrait of a fascinating Christian intellectual, warmly human, devoted to his Church in stormy weather and profoundly pastoral 'and it was the glory of this great man, to be thought a Christian, and whatever you added to it, he looked upon as a term of diminution'. It is not difficult to see why he cast a spell on those who knew him and on those who read him. He is rich in imagery and fancy but equally rich in spirituality and religious practicality. Perhaps this is the place to remind those who today may find the three nineteenth-century editions inaccessible that my friend T.K. Carroll has provided an excellent choice in his *Jeremy Taylor: Selected Works* (1990) in the series, Classics of Western Spirituality (Paulist Press, New York).

TAYLOR AND THE ANGLICAN ETHOS

Let me now try to outline briefly the climate in which Taylor's theological formation took place. That which is distinctive and characteristic in Anglicanism is not a theological system associated with one great name, such as Jean Calvin and his *Institutes* in Calvinism or, to a lesser degree, Aquinas and his *Summa* in Roman Catholicism. What is distinctively Anglican is not a theology but a theological method, the threefold appeal to Scripture, tradition and reason by means of which Anglicans test the authenticity of a Church, or a dogma or a doctrinal opinion. The absence of what might be termed a particular theology is deliberate for Anglicans have always stressed the *hapax* of the epistle of Jude - 'the faith once for all delivered'. Tradition is then the living Church interpreting the given faith in the idiom of each generation and conformably with the original revelation in Scripture. It is the expression of the Spirit *iuvenescens* (as Irenaeus put it), for the Spirit abides in the Church. Anglicans have always regarded the faith and order of the undivided Church of the first five centuries as being in some way normative, centuries in which the credal summaries were the rule of faith. The use of this threefold methodolgy allowed for, and in fact required, the distinction between fundamentals and matters of secondary importance. This too has historically been a characteristic of Anglicanism and was so noted in the *Malta Report* of JPARC in 1968.

So, what I am saying by way of examining the method and the direction of Jeremy Taylor's whole theological synthesis is that in this respect he is totally at one with the Anglican ethos whose 'distinctiveness lies in method rather than in content, for Anglicanism, as Chillingworth put it, has declined to call any man master in theology. There is no specifically Anglican corpus of doctrine (apart from Scripture and the faith of the Primitive Church) and no kingpin in Anglican theology such as Calvin,

Plate 4. Frontispiece, engraved by Hertochs, The Worthy Communicant.
First edition, London, 1660. (Lisburn Museum).

The Worthy

COMMUNICANT

OR

A Discourse of the Nature, Effects, and Blessings consequent to the worthy receiving of the

LORDS SUPPER

And of all the duties required in order to a worthy preparation:

Together

With the *Cases of Conscience* occurring in the duty of him that *Ministers* and of him that *Communicates*.

To which are added

Devotions fitted to every part of the Ministration.

By *Jeremy Taylor* D. D. *and Bishop Elect* of *Down* and *Connor*.

---

c d

LONDON,

Printed by *R. Norton* for *John Martin*, *James Allestry*, and *Thomas Dicas* at the *Bell* in *St. Pauls Church-yard*, 1660.

Plate 5. Title page, The Worthy Communicant. First edition, London, 1660. (Lisburn Museum).

nor is there any tendency to centralize more marginal doctrines such as predestination, nor to emphasize specific philosophies, such as Thomism or nominalism or any other one of the several brands of medieval philosophy'. (9) Perhaps it is not tendentious to describe the Anglican ethos as undifferentiated Catholicism which has passed through and profited by the experience of both the Renaissance and the Reformation. It is both Catholic and Reformed, stressing alike identity with and continuity with the faith and order of the Early Church and rejecting on the basis of the threefold appeal what it regards as additions to the faith once for all given. Within these parameters is a liberality in respect of opinions and affirmations of faith which are secondary or accessory to the fundamentals. Party terms are a 19th century anachronism, but using them as shorthand, one could say that Anglicanism is Evangelical in its proclamation of the centrality of the person of Jesus, the living Lord, and Catholic in its insistence on the Word and Sacraments as essential instruments in the transmission of His risen life to the members of His mystical Body, the Church. Both emphases are everywhere in Taylor and are the substance of his work.

HIS THEOLOGICAL METHOD: CONTEXT AND CONTENT

To place Taylor in this overall context we have but to turn to his writings. The threefold appeal is basic to his theology as for example in *The Real Presence and Spiritual of Christ in the Blessed Sacrament* (1654) where the whole structure of the book is to test eucharistic doctrines against the criteria of Scripture, the Fathers, reason and sense, ending with a careful critique of the doctrine of the Primitive Church. Similarly, in his great work on moral theology *Ductor Dubitantium* (1660), he rejects that kind of moral theology which 'was made a trade of the house, and an art of the schools' and instead seeks 'to show men the right paths of salvation; to describe the right and plain measures of simplicity'. To achieve this, he writes, 'I have begun an institution of moral theology' in which 'I affirm nothing but upon grounds of Scripture, or universal tradition, or right reason' (*The Preface*). As in his eucharistic theology and his moral theology, Taylor's procedure in his *Of the Sacred Order and Offices Of Episcopacy* (1642) is exactly the same as he endeavours to demonstrate that reason endorses the claim that Scripture and antiquity indicate clearly that 'episcopacy is not less than an apostolical ordinance' (Sect. XIX). Though it is everywhere in Taylor's work, let us meet this identical theological method set out, for my final example, at the close of *Clerus Domini* (1651) where the criteria showing 'the divine institution and necessity of the office ministerial' are set out: 'by the word of God, by the practice of the apostles, by the practice of sixteen ages of the Catholic Church, by the necessity of the thing, by reason' (VIII (18)). This, of course, is still the official stance of the Church of Ireland set out in the Preamble and Declaration. After asserting that the Church holds the Scripture as 'containing all things necessary to salvation' it goes on 'and doth continue to profess the faith of Christ as professed by the primitive Church'. It reflects the canon of 1571 which directed the clergy not to teach anything 'except what is agreeable to the doctrine of the Old and New Testaments and what the Catholic Fathers and ancient bishops have collected from the same doctrine'. Nor is this antiquarianism and I draw your attention to Canon A5 of the Church of England; 'The doctrine of the Church of England is grounded in the holy Scriptures, and in such teachings of the ancient Fathers and Councils of the Church as are agreeable to the said Scriptures. In particular such doctrine is to be found in the thirty-nine Articles of Religion, the Book of Common Prayer and the Ordinal'.

RULES
AND
ADVICES
To the Clergy
OF THE
DIOCESSE
OF
DOWN and *CONNER*,

For their Deportment in their Perſonal and Publick Capacities.

Given by *Jer. Taylor*, Biſhop of that Dioceſs, at the Viſitation at *LISNEGARVEY*.

The ſecond Edition.

LONDON:
Printed by *J. G.* for *Richard Royſton*, Bookſeller to the Kings moſt Excellent Majeſty, 1663.

Plate 6. Title page, Advices to the Clergy, given in 1661 at Lisnegarvey (Lisburn). Second edition, London, 1663. (Lisburn Museum).

This is in fact how Jeremy Taylor does theology and now when we find him saying 'Scripture, tradition, councils, and fathers are the evidence in a question, but reason is the judge' (X,5) then we find ourselves beginning to glimpse the individuality of Taylor as a theologian and his independence, his 'largeness of spirit' within the forward sweep of the threefold appeal. For now we see the theologian in the process of applying the method, grappling with the requirements of reason, with the limitations of the appeal to antiquity, with the mistaking of the range of the appeal to Scripture, and with the nature of fundamentals. The quotation I have just given is from Section X (5) of The *Liberty of Prophesying* (1647). This is, in my view, one of the books in which we can most clearly discern the essential Taylor, orthodox yet questioning, rejecting always those who 'allow us to be Christians and disciples, if we will lay aside our reason, which is that guard of our souls'. (10) It is significant that those words are from the *Ductor* not *The Liberty* for Taylor's theology is all of one piece as far as basics are concerned. Of course, when attempting an overview of a great Christian intellectual who has also a prodigious, output, we are always at risk of making snap judgments. Taylor himself was rather caustic about those who, as he put it, 'read three pages . . . after dinner' to inform themselves about an author. It is fatally easy because of the way in which, with learning, acuity and perception, Taylor immerses himself in any one given subject or area, effortlessly expounding and evaluating it, so that we are apt to forget the enormous range of his interests and his versatility. All the time we have to bear in mind that the man who writes with authority on the eucharist, on priesthood and episcopacy and who is the major practitioner in the restructuring of Anglican moral theology, is also a liturgist and a profoundly devotional writer whose main concern is with practical religion, 'making religion the business of our lives', 'the sanctification of the whole man', 'to advance the necessity, and to declare the manner and parts, of a good life', 'to imitate the holy Jesus'. Constantly he emphasises practicality in religion always relating it to 'the new life' and to the means of grace in Word and Sacrament. (11) One could go on and on but what I am trying to convey is some sort of sense of Taylor in the round, some sort of impression of his whole theological synthesis of which I am endeavouring to present a series of mere snapshots. My hope is that these will transmit a valid image of his esprit large within the Great Tradition in which his thought is saturated.

THE FUNCTIONING OF HIS THEOLOGY

So, it may illuminate our understanding of Jeremy Taylor, Anglican theologian, to glance at his handling of the four matters I raised a few minutes ago, and for the sake of brevity, do so largely from that one book *The Liberty of Prophesying* and begin with 'reason'. George Rust said Taylor would never allow himself to be governed by anything but reason and it is indeed a core-value in his theology. For him it is not a cold rationalism because he has learnt differently from the Cambridge Platonists. It is, he says, 'a transcendent that runs through all topics' and 'it is not guided by natural arguments only but by revelation and all other good means'. It may err and be inculpable. 'He seems' says Stranks 'to mean by 'reason', the exercise in judgment of all a man's powers, both spiritual and mental'.(12) These observations are from the *Liberty* (X,(5)) and are designed to show the authority of reason in any controversy – 'If we must judge, then we must use our reason' (ib) – 'for reason, like logic, is instrument of all things else; and when revelation, and philosophy, and public experience, and all other grounds of probability or demonstration, have supplied us with matter, then reason does but make use of them'. Personality and capacity are involved.

> 'That which will demonstrate a truth to one person, possibly will never move another. Because our reason does not consist in a mathematical point; and the heart of reason, that vital and most sensible part, in which only it can be conquered fairly, is an ambulatory essence, and not fixed; it wanders up and down like a floating island, or like that which we call the life-blood'.

Indeed in the *Ductor* (Bk II, C.I. Rule I) he likens reason to 'a box of quicksilver' or 'a dove's neck, or a changeable taffata; it looks to me otherwise than to you, who do not stand in the same light that I do'.

What we are looking at is a Christian intellectual – curiously modern in some ways – who while rejecting an omnipotent, self-illuminating reason, firmly holds that reason, truly informed, Spirit guided, is indeed 'the candle of the Lord'. 'Right reason' he says 'is not the positive and affirmative measure of any article, yet it is the negative measure of every one'. In other words 'whatsoever is contradictory to right reason, is at no hand to be admitted as a mystery of faith'. He even affirms that while you cannot prove the deepest articles of faith 'by natural reason' any more than you can prove them.

> 'By arithmetic or rules of music; [yet] whosoever believes wisely and not by chance, enters into his faith by the hand of reason; that is, he hath causes and reasons why he believes, indeed not wisely, but for some reason or other he does it'.

This is really no different from Austin Farrer in our own day saying that 'if we are persuaded some element of faith is there'. Taylor's conclusion is striking when he writes in the *Ductor* (II, Rule III C.24) that 'If I find that all things satisfy my reason, I believe him saying that God said so; and then *pistis* or faith enters'. He enters some caveats, such as that a thing ought not to be suspect because it is above the understanding. Also, it is unsafe to conclude that because a thing is agreeable to right reason it is necessarily so in Scripture, and he instances the repelling of force by force. There is a humility here, an awareness of human limitations even when reason is being carefully guarded which has no point of contact with a self-sufficient idea of the function and capacity of reason: 'there is' he says 'a *ragione di stato*, and a *ragione di regno*, and a *ragione di cielo*, after which none but fools will inquire, and none but the humble shall ever find'.(13)

In other words, as Taylor uses the threefold appeal we are not looking at a theologian who regards these criteria as a sort of magic holdall or as a rule of thumb to be applied uncritically and which automatically produces right doctrine – a penny-in-the-slot theology. Rather are the criteria to be used to ensure right direction, but with freedom and flexibility. Taylor firmly believes, as does R. P. C. Hanson, that 'we cannot start Christianity again from a *tabula rasa*, nor from the Bible alone, nor wholly and consistently from any past point in history . . . but we must be prepared to reexamine and reassess tradition'.[14]

We can see the same quality in Taylor's application of the appeal to Scripture and to tradition, and we begin to see that he is a theologian – not simply a propounder of dogma but a searcher into the truth of dogma. For him, the threefold appeal is an essential signpost but not an ordinance-survey map. It is therefore not surprising that he approves the work of the liberal Dutch jurist and theologian, Hugo Grotius. Interestingly, I recently came across an instance of Grotius being required reading for Anglican ordinands as late as 1848.[15] Taylor's own liberality is set out in the Epistle Dedicatory of the *Liberty*: 'this unity is to be estimated according to the unity of faith, in things necessary, in matters of creed, and articles fundamental: for as for other things, it is more to be wished than to be hoped for'. In fact, says Taylor, most of the disunity and dissension is caused when men call 'superstructures by the name of fundamental articles' and this distinction is everywhere in his writings.

Of course, the *Liberty* got him into trouble as so often happens to exponents of charity and toleration. The same liberality appears in his application of the appeal to Scripture and to tradition. Obviously, he is deeply committed in both cases but what we are looking at here in Taylor is the rejection of the fundamentalism of his own times in respect both of Scripture and of tradition – the biblical infallibilism of the sects of the magisterial infallibilism of the papacy. There is all the difference in the world between traditionalism and what Michael Ramsey once called 'the intelligent appeal to tradition'. In fact the one is the dead hand of the past while the other is a life-line. Nor, to quote Ramsey again is 'Scripturalism the same thing as the appeal to Holy Scripture'.[16] Taylor refused both fundamentalisms. Deeply committed to the appeal to tradition as an integral element in the Anglican ethos, he, and his peers, were alive to its limits and insisted that tradition had to be conformable to Scripture and amenable to reason. Taylor was vastly learned in patristics, basic to his book on episcopacy (1642) and to his eucharistic theology in *The Real Presence and Spiritual* (1654). But like the members of the Tew Circle he freely admitted to being influenced by Jean Daillé's book so that his oft-expressed veneration for the Fathers is informed by a critical modernity. This new historical criticism was a development advanced by Daillé's *Traicté de l'employ des Saints péres* which demonstrated that to expect patristic unanimity was a non-starter: the Anglicans and Taylor never thought that they provided unanimity. Rather did they regard the Fathers as valuable corroborators of Scripture and venerable interpreters of the Faith 'once for all delivered', as Taylor pointed out in a second dedication when the *Liberty* (1647), *Episcopacy Asserted* (1642) and his *Apology for Authorized and Set Forms of Liturgie* (1649) were reissued in a single volume: 'The saying of the fathers alone is no demonstration of faith'.(17) Tradition then is no ultimate or independent guarantor of faith and praxis though 'there are some that think they can determine all questions in the world by two or three sayings of the Fathers, or by the consent of so many as they will please to call a concurrent testimony'.(18) He sums up his view of the question in that memorable phrase: 'Scripture, tradition, councils, and fathers are the *evidence* in a question, but reason is the judge'.(19)

Perhaps I have gone some way to showing that in Taylor's theologizing – how glad I am that the dictionary now allows that useful word – the basic Anglican ethos is set forth but with an independence, an individuality, which is as attractive as it is striking in that, at times, he seems to belong to our age as well as to his own.

A

SERMON

Preached in *Christs-Church Dublin,*
July 16. 1663.

AT THE FUNERAL

Of the most Reverend Father in God,

JOHN,

Late Lord Archbishop of Armagh, *and*
Primate of all Ireland:

WITH

A succinct Narrative of his whole Life.

The third Edition, enlarged.

By the Right Reverend Father in God,
JEREMY,
Lord Bishop of Down *and* Connor.

LONDON:
Printed by *J. G.* for *Richard Royston,* Bookseller to the
Kings most Excellent Majesty, 1663.

Plate 7. Title page, A Sermon preached at the funeral of John Bramhall, Archbishop of Armagh, 16th July 1663. Third edition, London, 1663. (Lisburn Museum).

Possibly then my best endeavour to transmit Taylor's originality is to comment briefly in conclusion on how this quality appears in his moral theology, his eucharistic writings, his views on original sin which also got him into trouble and on his outstanding contribution as a devotional writer. He himself, having left us fifteen volumes, each averaging five to six hundred pages, would have looked askance at such brevity of treatment – but the occasion requires it and our human weakness demands it! Each subject is matter for a book, a full-length portrait, but today I am in the business of producing snap-shots.

As to moral theology, the first thing to realise is that the Anglicans restructured the science by merging into one spiritual instrument moral theology and ascetical theology – long separated with unfortunate results. Led by Sanderson and developed by Taylor moral theology for Anglicans became the science of Christian living – 'the art of full co-operation with grace, in a total Christian life. It emphasized progress towards perfection rather than keeping on the right side of the law'.(20) What in fact, they were doing was re-siting moral theology within the kerygmatic totality of the Gospel – 'if any one is in Christ, he is a new creation' (2 Cor. 5:17) and this *kainē ktisis* is central to Taylor's writing on the subject, and indeed to his preaching. The remarkable thing is that Anglican moral theology thus restructured anticipated the total transformation of moral theology which came about in the science as outlined by Roman Catholic and Anglican moralists from the 1940's onwards. This was a quiet revolution in which can be seen the familiar emphases of Taylor, Sanderson and others. 'We understand moral theology as the doctrine of the imitation of Christ, as the life in, with, and through Christ'. It might be Taylor speaking but in fact it is the leading Roman Catholic moralist of our times, Bernard Häring. (21) When in a later book, his *Medical Ethics* (1972), Häring insists that, rather than being a soul imprisoned in a sinful body, 'Man is an embodied spirit . . . the specific nature of man lies in his being, through his bodily existence open to the Other, to the 'we' of the community and the world around him' (pp. 21, 45, 50-51), we find that Taylor as it were in anticipation has had a similar intuition about the human condition. In *The Great Exemplar* (*Works*, II, pp. 168-169), though he agrees with the traditional view that 'the body is the instrument of sins' he also writes 'the body is the shop and forge for the soul, in which all her designs, which are transient upon external objects are framed' and 'the body', he avers, 'is organical and instrumental to the soul'. There is a sort of prophetic depth at times in Taylor which brings one up short in contemplation and assessment of a remarkable theologian who values the tradition with its valid implications but who is not locked into it. The Caroline stress on repentance as *metanoia* is central instead of the concept of penance and we find the whole range of the Caroline reforms in place today. Taylor's contribution to the subject was large and original. His *Unum Necessarium* (1655) set out the nature and practice of repentance which he calls 'a whole state of the new life, an entire change', the response and responsibility which lie at the heart of *metanoia.* This revisionism is reflected in modern moral theology. Having written at length on this subject elsewhere, I must be careful to content myself with noting the books in which he made an individual contribution to what was, I believe, his main preoccupation in theology, moral/ascetical theology.(22) He himself called it 'that part of theology which is most necessary . . . a whole body of practical divinity, in which the life of religion and of all our hopes depend'.(23) In fact, he and his friend Rust considered his huge work on conscience and casuistry, the *Ductor Dubitantium* (1660) to be his greatest and most lasting achievement. But his first major work *The Great Exemplar* (1649) is full of this fresh, restructured 'practical divinity' as our ancestors termed moral theology.

In the same way his best known work today, his *Holy Living* (1650) is in reality a book of applied moral/ascetical theology for the ordinary practising Christian. With genius, Taylor marries practical divinity with a tender but unsentimental devotional spirit so that one can appreciate Gosse's view that he was 'the most gracious voice then to be heard in England'. In Taylor, the originality here is the combination of artistry, imagination and vision with a down-to-earth religion for Monday mornings. Even in this area Taylor's integrity as a theologian got him into trouble again. His *Unum Necessarium* (1655) is a great practical and devotional work on central aspects of moral theology but Chapter VI contained a time-bomb which exploded into controversy, earning for him titles such as semi-Pelagian and even Socinian. The cause of the rumpus was the sanity of Taylor's views on original sin and the vast simplicity of common-sense in his understanding of the human condition. He confronted head-on the current contemporary Augustinianism with its determinism and Taylor insists that original sin has not impaired man's freedom of choice, though it is a contagion: 'Adam had liberty of choice and chose ill and so do we'. The Fall left mankind 'in pure naturals', but 'mere nature brings not to hell, but choice'. Augustinianism is unscriptural: 'Could we prevent the sin of Adam? could we hinder it? Were we ever asked?'(24) The Fathers support him, Taylor claims, and I draw your attention to the fact that it was Augustine who gave currency to the non-Scriptural term 'peccatum originale', turning the reasonably optimistic patristic view of human nature as suffering *deprivation* (Tertullian speaks of 'vitium originis') into *depravation* through the Fall. It is fascinating but I must stop, simply underlining Taylor's constant liberality, as I have termed it. He himself said of this controversy 'men are angry at my ingenuity (i.e. ingenuousness) and openness of discourse'.(25)

EUCHARISTIC THEOLOGY AND LITURGY

I close this overlong lecture with a cursory glance at Taylor's eucharistic theology. You will find it in his *The Real Presence and Spiritual of Christ in the Blessed Sacrament* (1654), in his *The Worthy Communicant* (1660), in Discourse XIX of *The Great Exemplar* (1649) and in Chapter IV, Section X of *Holy Living* (1650). Here again, books have been written on Taylor's thinking about the eucharist,(26) All I may allow myself here is to signalize briefly what appears to me to be central to his thought. A devoted Anglican, he remains always his own man and on this subject too he resists the classification to which later generations have become accustomed. His doctrine of the real spiritual presence having also an undertone of virtualism, a matter which would reappear again in the 1938 report *Doctrine in the Church of England.*

It is enough for me to remind you that mystery is Taylor's fundamental concept in thinking about the eucharist. It is a mystery of light: 'Christ comes to meet us, clothed with a mystery'; 'The sacraments are mysteries' and everywhere the eucharist is 'this mystery which is both sacrament and sacrifice' and the elements are 'the holy mysteries'. His favourite theme of 'Christ who is our life', 'the new creation', is deeply embedded in his picture of what happens at Holy Communion for the mystery of the eucharist merges essentially with morality and Christian behaviour: 'if I describe our duty, it plainly signifies the greatness and excellency of the mystery . . . and we cannot draw all the lines of duty, but so much duty must needs open a cabinet of mysteries'. He never allows us to forget that he is a moral theologian. Of the elements he constantly speaks of 'that great mysteriousness which is the sacramental change', not physical 'but figurative, mysterious, and sacramental'. 'It is bread, and it is Christ's body. It is bread in substance, Christ in the sacrament . . . the first substance is changed by grace, but remains the same in nature'. What Taylor has to say on the mystery of the presence and the mystery of the sacrifice is profoundly illuminating and creative for today's theologian and today's communicant.

Nor is this all, for Taylor was also a liturgist and composed *A Collection of Offices* (1658) for use since the Prayer Book of the persecuted Church had been proscribed and suppressed. This whole new liturgy was a unique initiative and achievement. Use was made of the Liturgies of St. James and of St. John Chrysostom and Taylor's use of acclamations foreshadows modern liturgical revisions as his 'Lord, I am not worthy that thou shouldest come under my roof' anticipates the modern Roman rite, 'Lord, I am not worthy to receive you'. Always, Taylor's modernity, his strange capacity of being at times ahead of his times, keeps surprising us at different levels of his output. Truly, he is a limitless man.(27)

Yet you will still not see the whole man unless you realize that this prodigious theologian, devotional teacher, liturgist and literary figure is also a deeply pastoral man, sought after as counsellor, confessor and preacher. The firm foundation of it all is the homely discipline and devotion of priesthood. He had set this out for his brethren in his *Clerus Domini* (1651), in *The Rules and Advices to the Clergy* (1661) and in *The Whole Duty of the Clergy* (1667). It is a picture of the clergyman as he should be seen in his parish, visiting the sick and the whole, familiar with the concerns of his people, counselling, advising, reconciling differences and solving difficulties, relieving the poor and needy – all within the framework of personal devotion built around the Daily Office. We remember that he died of a fever contracted when sick-visiting in Lisburn, priest and pastor to the end. His advice to his colleagues mirrors his personal practice as recorded by George Rust. For Jeremy Taylor, spiritual experience, practical divinity and theology are necessarily inseparable and mutually supportive in the exercise of our Christian calling and in the discharge of the ministerial office. [(28)] Was it not the point made by George Herbert in that lovely poem *The Windows* when he wrote:

'Doctrine and life, colours and
light, in one
When they combine and
mingle, bring
A strong regard and awe'

So, I draw to a close.

'The Glory of God is the living man;
And the life of man is the Vision of God'

I think that Taylor would allow me those word from Irenaeus, whose writings he knew,[(29)] and who, separated from him by fourteen centuries, was near to him in the fundamentals of faith and spirituality.

H. R. McADOO

Du&tor Dubitantium,

OR

THE RULE

OF

CONSCIENCE

In all her

GENERAL MEASURES;

Serving as a great Inſtrument for the determination of

Caſes of Conſcience.

In Four Books. The Third Edition.

By *JEREMY TAYLOR*, Chaplain in Ordinary to King *CHARLES* the Firſt
and late Lord Biſhop of *Down* and *Conner*.

Prov. 14. 8.

Σοφία πανέργων ἐπιγνώσεται τὰς ὁδοὺς αὐτῶν· ἄνοια δὲ ἀφρόνων ἐν πλάνῃ.

LONDON, Printed by *R. Norton*, for *R. Royſton*, Bookſeller to the King's
moſt Sacred Majeſty, M DC LXXVI.

Plate 8. Title page, Ductor Dubitantium. Book for moral guidance completed during Taylor's refuge at Portmore, near Lisburn. Engraved by Peter Lombart. Third edition, London, 1673. (Lisburn Museum).

NOTES

(1) Taylor's *Works.* (Vol. I, Heber ed., p. ccciii).
(2) Edmund Gosse, *Jeremy Taylor* (1904), pp. 58-60.
(3) C. J. Stranks, *The Life and Writings of Jeremy Taylor* (1952), p. 273.
(4) During his time as Bishop Down and Connor.
(5) See *Works,* Vol. I, pp. 4-24.
(6) This and subsequent quotations from Rust's funeral sermon, *Works* (ed. Heber), Vol. I.
(7) From *The Golden Grove* (1930), the Introduction by Logan Pearsall Smith. See also my *First of Its Kind: Jeremy Taylor's Life of Christ* (1994), pp.62-73.
(8) Alec R. Vidler, *Essays in Liberality* (1957), pp. 21-22.
(9) cp. H. R. McAdoo *The Spirit of Anglicanism* (1965), Introduction and Chap. I.
(10) *Doctor Dubitantium*, Bk. I, C.I, Rule III (19): Heber ed. Vol. XI, p. 439.
(11) *Works,* Vol. VI, P.6; vol. II, Preface pp. 1v-1vi, Preface to *The Great Exemplar;*
(12) C. J. Stranks, loc. cit., p. 308.
(13) H. R. McAdoo, *The Spirit of Anglicanism* (1965), pp. 59-60.
(14) R.P.C. Hanson *Continuity of Christian Doctrine* (1981), pp. 82-3, 88.
(15) John Breay, *A Fell-Side Parson* (1995), p. 11.
(16) Michael Ramsey, *The Anglican Spirit* (ed. Dale Coleman, 1991), pp. 34, 150
(17) Taylor, *Works,* Vol. VII, p. xviii..
(18) *Liberty,* Sect. VIII (1) ; Works, Vol. VIII, p. 78.
(19) *Liberty*, Sect. X (5).
(20) Martin Thornton, *English Spirituality* (1963), p. 239..
(21) *The Law of Christ* (1959), I, p. 61.
(22) See my *The Structure of Caroline Moral Theology* (1949); my 'Anglican Moral Theology in the Seventeenth Century: An Anticipation' in *The Anglican Moral Choice* (ed. Paul Elmen, 1983) and my *First of Its Kind*: *Jeremy Taylor's Life of Christ* (1994).
(23) *Unum Necessarium,* Preface and Ch. III, Sect. I, Taylor Works, Vol. VIII, pp. ccxliii, 337.
(24) *Unum Necessarium*, Ch. VI, Section IV, (67), Section I (36) and Ch. VII, Section IV (16).
(25) Introductory letter to *Deus Justificatus* (1656).
(26) See passages in C.J. Stranks's *The Life and Writings of Jeremy Taylor* (1952) and my *The Eucharistic Theology of Jeremy Taylor Today* (1988). See also H.R. McAdoo and Kenneth Stevenson, *The Mystery of the Eucharist in the Anglican Tradition* (1995) and Kenneth Stevenson, *Covenant of grace Renewed* (1994).
(27) This aspect of Taylor's work is examined by Harry Boone Porter in his *Jeremy Taylor, Liturgist* (1979).
(28) See H. R. McAdoo, 'The Whole Duty of the Clergy' in *SEARCH*, 1993 (Vol.16,No-One).
(29) In his *Dissuasive* (1664), Part II, Section II and IV, Taylor shows Anglican agreement with Irenaeus on the total sufficiency of the Scriptures who wrote 'We have received the economy of our salvation by no other but by those', and with Irenaeus on 'the tradition of truth' which is 'that tradition apostolical': Taylor, *Works,* Vol. X, pp. 394-5, 459-460.

This book can be obtained from the

Church of Ireland Historical Society,

c/o:- The Rev. Dr. W. G. Neely,
The Rectory,
Crossmore Road,
Keady,
Co. Armagh BT60 3JY